Brooks B

D0628188

Understanding Millennials

Tips and Tricks for Working with
Today's Generation

Adam Brooks

Copyright © 2016 Adam Brooks

ISBN-10:099745850X

ISBN-13: 978-09974585-0-3

Dedication

To all my friends and family who thought I was crazy to leave steady employment to chase my dreams of consulting and speaking, to those who let me crash in their guest bedrooms, those who made me a home-cooked meal, and to those who sent encouraging notes, I couldn't have done any of the things I've been able to do without you! This is also for my family, who always gives me inspiration and crazy stories to tell from the stage.

Table of Contents

Preface

I received my bachelor's degree in Speech Communications. Once I finished my undergrad, I began working at Remuda Ranch an internationally renowned eating disorder/anxiety clinic. During that time I received my first graduate degree, a Masters of Arts in Education with an emphasis in special education. I quickly got into education where I became the Director of Special Education for an inner city high school. During that time, I received my second graduate degree, this time in leadership development. I taught and worked with teens in the school system for over ten years, also working as a seasonal camp director for four of those years. Currently I am an adjunct Professor at a local community college and at a major university. For the last 6 years I have been traveling and speaking to camps, schools, and conferences about a variety of issues facing us today. You'd think I'd be used to speaking in front of an audience.

I was asked to speak at a luncheon last year, the topic: how to apply the work I've done with teens to business professionals. This stressed me out in the beginning. I'm used to cracking jokes about pop culture or using words like "ratchet" or "fleek." I wasn't sure I would have much of value to offer an audience full of business people. The feeling dissipated as soon as I finished my overview of what I do and an explanation of the book I co-wrote, *WTF —Why Teens Fail and What to Fix*. I was surprised to find that I had a room full of professionals, with most of their hands raised high, waiting to ask questions: "Why are teens so lazy?", "How come the young people I work with seem to not have the same work ethic that I had when I was younger?", "My kid just plays his video games all day. How can I get him to stop?", "Can you tell me why my workers keep fighting over text messages when they are at work? I need that to change!"

That's when I decided that I needed to devote my time to trying to help bridge the gap between Millennials and the generation that is managing and working with them on a daily basis. I am not here to judge which generation is right or wrong…every generation thinks they do things better than the others. My goal is to define ways that we can increase the productivity of Millennials, and therefore, add benefits to modern businesses. If this generation really is as large as the stats and data say, then changing all of them will be much harder than if we simply change our management and business practices.

Cheers, and I hope you enjoy my suggestions on how to help the current generation find their best practices for work and life. I hope you also learn, as I have, how great their potential really is. Chelsea Clinton took the words right out of my mouth…

"Millennials are often portrayed as apathetic, disinterested, tuned out and selfish. None of those adjectives describe the Millennials I've been privileged to meet and work with."—Chelsea Clinton

Where Have They Been?

"My Momma Told Me So!"

When we talk about the millennial generation, typically we mean anyone born after 1985. But there are differing opinions about what makes someone a Millennial:

They're unique from being raised around technology!

No! It's because they were born in the 90's!

A lot of people want to break the generation up into subgroups, but, for the sake of this mini-book, when we say "Millennial" we mean anyone born between 1985 and 2004.

In the last 20 years, we have seen the development of a new generation that has had a very different upbringing than any other generation before it. Ever heard the phrase "helicopter parenting"? It's a change in raising children that has helped shape the whole generation. Helicopter parenting is best described as the parents of the child being so concerned with the child's well-being that they literally "hover" over all aspects of the child's life to make sure that he doesn't get hurt or make bad decisions. Due to the parent always being present, the child is often unaccustomed to being told "no" or that they are wrong. Stereotypically, these parents don't believe that their child does anything wrong and, if an issue arises, it has to be the fault of someone other than their child. As a former school teacher, as much as I wish this was an exaggeration, I heard the following statements more often than not:

"My kid would never do that."

"You must be thinking of someone else, I know my kid better than you do."

Did you know that the term "helicopter parent" originated in the late 60's when a young kid told therapist-turned-author Dr. Haim Ganott, "My mom just hovers over me like a helicopter"?

The result is learned helplessness on the part of the child. Kids with parents like these typically haven't learned how to struggle for anything they have nor have they had to do anything to develop emotionally and socially, which has left their socioemotional growth stunted.

The long-term effects of restricted socioemotional growth appear to be the inability to work through tough situations on their own, a tendency to struggle to gain and hold down employment, and the continuous pursuit of "the helicopter" to fix most, if not all, of their problems. Something as simple as always being there for your kid and never letting him struggle can really have an adverse effect when he is older.

"All Men Are Created Equal, So I Can Do What I Want, Right?"

What this generation holds dear is equality for all. It is something that other generations have strived for throughout history. With this generation, though there is a difference: They know what it's like to have equality. They all got trophies just for participating in sports while growing up. No matter how they did on the team or how well their team did, everyone was awarded a trophy or ribbon. This credo of "no matter how hard you try, everyone gets the same treatment" helped shape the idea of equality for this generation.

Some people, who seem to be extreme, have said this attitude is "creating Socialists." However, I think it's more complex than that. I do see that everyone wants to be treated equally: whether they are the janitor, CEO, or general employee. This sense of equality runs deep. An example is a Millennial who suddenly has a great idea or needs something so he bursts into the CEO's office demanding to see them. A sense of equality, and of the right to assert it, can cross boundaries from home to work quickly—another Millennial trait.

This abrasiveness is not something that generations past are used to; typically, non-Millennials have a firm distinction in place between what's appropriate at work and what is not. The lines are blurry with this younger generation. To their way of thinking, there is no such thing as tiers or levels in jobs or life. Because they want something just as much as the people above them, they believe they should have access to it.

Currently there are 40 million Millennials in the workplace!

The way this equal-access notion most typically shows up in the lives of kids is when they apply for their dream job, which they may or may not be qualified for, and are devastated when they don't get it. Now to be honest this is normal...most of us would be devastated if we didn't get our dream job. However, most of us would not apply for our dream job right out of college or after high school. We would work up to that dream job, we would work entry-level positions in order to get promoted to our dream job.

This doesn't always seem to be an option for Millennials. I have seen many students who didn't get the perfect job right away decide to settle for something completely different. Instead of getting a lower job in the same field and working toward their dream position, they were willing to chuck the whole career out of the window and bounce to a different field.

It is possible that this behavior is about an issue with equality, but it could also be a product of the Attention Deficit Disorder (ADD) epidemic that this generation is experiencing. I worked as the director of special education at a high school for almost 10 years. I know that ADD is real, and kids need medication for it at times. I have witnessed it in action firsthand. I don't throw that term around lightly.

However, I do think that this generation has an attention problem. They feel more comfortable flitting from one activity to another than sitting and working on one thing all day. They prefer jobs like sales or hospitality services because each day is unique, unlike the one before, but even these jobs seem to get boring for Millennials after a while. The idea of being a specialist in one specific field doesn't seem near as much fun as knowing a little bit about a ton of different topics.

We need to teach Millennials that while all men are created equal in opportunity, it is what they do with that opportunity that sets them apart.

"Wanna Get Married? What's Your Name Again?"

My last year teaching high school, I was asked to teach a senior English class. Something I noticed about the students was that they knew intimate details about each other's lives. When they would tease or say mean things, their comments would pack a punch because they knew right where to hit one another—what to say that would trigger the harshest response. So how did they find out about these very intimate life details? From each other!

The issue here is that Millennials don't understand the concept of appropriate self-disclosure. Something that I didn't even learn about until I was in college. There are appropriate ways, places, and times for telling someone about yourself. When we first meet someone, it is not considered entirely appropriate to tell them, "Hi, I'm divorced and my husband cheated on me…" For most of us, this is common sense. We would never tell anyone this on our first meeting. However, to think this is common sense for everyone is simply not true.

Knowing what, where, and when to disclose personal information is a skill that has to be learned and developed over time. Once we decide that someone is worthy of having that personal information about us, then we decide whether to share with them or not. It is a process that happens gradually with many meetings and encounters, not instantaneously. We build a relationship before we share intimate details about our lives. It is a give-and-take thing. The more we spend time with someone, the more we will inevitably share, the more we share, the closer we get. It has to take time, otherwise we can fall off that balancing beam. When we share too much too soon, we risk the other person having valuable information they can use against us because they are still deciding whether or not they like us and want us in their circle. Let's say they do not want us in their circle, they now have tons of ammunition to use against us in social settings. The opposite is true as well: if we spend time with people and never learn something new about them, we never feel close to them, and therefore, we never really get to value the relationship.

Did you know that U.S. Millennials touch their smartphones 45 times a day?

Along with how we learn about each other, we also have appropriate places to learn that information. Traditionally, having friends in the workplace hasn't been the norm. There has been an unspoken separation between work and play. People at work might like and talk to each other casually but rarely know a lot of intimate details about one another; this is in contrast to how people interact with friends in their personal lives, friends that are invited over for barbecues or out for drinks. Colleagues and friends, stereotypically, have been different sets of people. But Millennials don't understand this separation. Due to this generation's inability to see boundaries as anything other than superficial, they share endless amounts of information upon the first meeting with anyone and everyone at work or outside of work. They so desire to be authentic and genuine, yet, because they have never really truly learned how to do so safely and appropriately, they are walking open books of all their deepest darkest secrets.

"Me Versus We"

When all these things are combined, Millennials have Veruca Salt syndrome. When I watched the movie Willy Wonka and the Chocolate Factory and saw the character Veruca Salt yell, "But I want it now DADDYYYYYYY!" I thought to myself, "Wow that is a beautiful depiction of a self-centered person!" However, I want to be careful here because a child who was helicopter parented displays this type of behavior. Listen to me now: *it is not the child's or younger person's fault!!*

Millennials never decided how they would be raised or what sort of world they would grow up in. Everything today is customized, from our phones to social media, even the cars we buy. Why shouldn't kids growing up today think that it's all about them? They should think that and they do. Yet we get frustrated and upset at them, which makes it even more confusing for them. They are living out what they know to be true. Their helicopter mom told them they were the most important thing in the world, so they aren't sure why *you* didn't get the memo! They want what they want and typically they want it NOW!

Where Are They Going?

"Let's light the world on fire!"

Now that we discussed some of the things that are trigger points for older generations who deal with Millennials, let's talk about where this generation is headed in life. At least in their opinions.

Millennials are considered the most philanthropic generation we have ever had. We have already seen a resurgence in social good works across the country. This generation has figured out ways to sell shoes in the United States, while simultaneously donating the same number of shoes to children in third-world countries who needed them. Millennials made donating eyeglasses to people around the world a popular endeavor. This generation would like to single-handedly end poverty, racism, and world hunger (as long as they don't get distracted)!

Their sense of equality makes Millennials extremely passionate about current social justice issues all over the globe. Since they have the Internet literally in the palms of their hands, they know about these issues in great detail as they happen. There are plenty of examples of young people getting involved in a variety of social causes. The backing of groups focused on helping various African countries and children there, Invisible Children and Falling Whistles are among the best examples.

This generation has raised more money than ever for causes, like Amyotrophic Lateral Sclerosis (ALS) research, the Pat Tillman Foundation, and social change. They have even financially fought rebels in African jungles. Their passion has been contagious and has inspired older generations to donate funds and resources to help these endeavors as well. The Millennials' passion for making changes can be infectious!

Keep in mind Millennials are the most educated generation in our history!

"Worlds Full of Entrepreneurs."

Thinking outside the box has to be brought up when we talk about this generation. However, I don't think Millennials have any concept of what that box is (that they aren't in). When we talk about people who think outside the box, they tend to be what we would call ultra-creative. Yet, this is typically news to them because they are only doing what makes sense to them.

What makes sense to Millennials may not make sense to us. Not because their thinking is inherently bad or wrong but because we understand the world differently. The new technology and helpful phone apps that are being created daily—that some of us would swear we can't live without—are mind-boggling. To think that we are creating truly efficient and environmentally conscious cars, for the first time, speaks to this change. We have innovation happening today, and for much of it we have to thank this generation.

We are even reinventing how we "do school" and teach. I have been in education for over 10 years. I have worked with people who thought that innovation was taking what we taught in the classroom and simply putting the same curriculum online. That couldn't be further from the truth. I have seen new schools created that are singularly focused and dedicated to success while, using things like consistent mentoring or mobile schooling, keeping kids constantly engaged. I even got to see a school that's solely focused and dedicated to empowering females in our male-dominated culture. These are true innovations that have started with the dawning of this millennial age.

The development of continual innovation goes past inventing for inventing's sake but rather is focused on the betterment of society, which really is exciting to see.

"Money Can't Buy Me Love!"

The reason that this generation believes that we are all equal is the exact same reason why they give money to someone at a bus stop. They believe that buying food for someone who can't afford it sort of balances the scales a bit. That's why a lot of people of older generations have called the Millennials "Socialists."

I'm not sure whether I agree or not. Millennials don't really have a concept of Communism or what a Socialist structure looks like. They aren't old enough to remember what the USSR is or to really understand what makes China different from the United States. Our youth today are world travelers, and yet they have not traveled anywhere to see it all. They can see so much from the comfort of their own bedroom.

They have seen what a lust for money does to people, and they want no part of it. They would much rather have a happy, healthy, and cohesive family unit than lots of money to buy whatever they want. I have met many students who were happy and content riding a bus every day to school as opposed to saving up for a car. They have seen rich celebrities go through marriage after marriage and sit on television telling people how depressed and unhappy they are. Money has never answered the question "How do you find happiness?" for this generation.

They do understand they need money to achieve certain tasks, but they also understand the power of how, and where, they spend their money. I know Millennials who refuse to spend money at places like Walmart or GAP. Why? Because the employment and purchasing practices of these companies conflict with their own personal values as individuals.

This group desires happiness and has found happiness in a small overcrowded house, surrounded by family and friends. They know it's there, and that's why they don't mind staying. The only reason this generation has a desire to make more money is to help the people they love and to do more good in this world. This is a generalization, but overwhelmingly, more members of this generation pursue happiness over making tons of money, because they don't believe that you can do both.

By 2018, Millennials will have the most spending power of any generation.

What Do We Do With Them?

Tips and Tricks: Ten easy things you can implement in your business to make it millennial friendly

1. Short-range goals

Because this generation is easily distracted, creating short achievable goals is a good way to help them become more productive. The more goals that are met, the better the worker feels, which instills more confidence and harder work. It can be a great cycle to get your workers in, once they buy into it.

We have all struggled under people who have high expectations. It's a mix of not wanting to disappoint your employer and worrying that you'll forget something that can be paralyzing. I would say that Millennials are not necessarily paralyzed, but rather they understand concepts differently from their employer. Having so much going on inside their brains, they struggle to work on long-view goals. Their brains are used to bouncing back and forth between processes and tasks that need their attention. They have survived with this short attention span their whole lives, and now they are asked to sit down and achieve one lengthy goal all by themselves.

One lengthy goal really is counterproductive for them. It will take them longer to perform this goal than it would if they were able to collaborate or if the assignment was broken up into smaller pieces and given out all at once so that they could bounce back and forth between each part of the task. When they had homework as kids they would bounce from math to English and back to math for a bit before getting their Spanish and health done. It was easier to let their brains flutter from task to task, and it enabled them to get it done faster.

Keep this in mind when you are assigning projects: Millennials will amaze you as long as you don't load them up from the beginning with assignments and goals that are long-term oriented. If you do that, you will receive the proverbial glassy-eyed look that teachers and parents know all too well when dealing with Millennials.

2. Opportunities for coaching and input

The Millennial generation wants to feel equal, so provide 360-degree coaching opportunities. Design a specific time and place for workers to get together and actually talk one-on-one about things that can better the company…whether it is what the bosses can do better, what their fellow employees can do better, or what someone underneath them can do better. This gives them a chance to be heard and allows bosses to have valuable feedback.

One-on-one time also allows Millennial employees to feel like the boss is being real, or authentic, in their interaction with them. This generation does not see themselves as independent; I mean they like their individualism, but they see themselves as part of a whole—a team or a brotherhood. Giving them access, even if it is limited, to someone who makes decisions can help them feel like they belong. When Millennials feel like their input matters and is listened to genuinely by their employers, then they gain a sense of belonging. This can be tricky because we are letting people coach others above them, below them and next to them.

First, we have to teach Millennials, give them a model and platform for how to do that. If we let them just tell anyone, anytime, what they should be doing differently, it can cause quite a bit of chaos. However, we could create an email address where everyone can shoot off suggestions that are appropriate, and then someone goes through that email once a week to see if there is anything of value. Or there could be a designated office and time where people could meet, chat, and share ideas of growth and coaching—that might also be a way it could work for a company. You really have to find a method that can work for your group specifically. The more guidelines and parameters you put on the sharing, though, the more the Millennials will feel like you aren't trusting them enough to coach appropriately.

So you have to brainstorm with your management team to find ways to give them freedom, yet let it still be calculated so that the process stays appropriate and worth the time.

3. Get real

Using terms that signal authenticity—like "I'm just going to be real" or "Can I be honest with you?"—can go a long way with Millennials. So use them often with this generation. Even if your message is simple and not that important, Millennials will still value that you are doing your best to be authentic and genuine with them. That will not only go a long way to gaining the Millenials trust but might make you a better manager.

Authenticity is not just a word that companies should throw around to sound more relevant. It's a quality that people notice, respond to, and respond out of. The term "authentic" may describe someone who simply shares too much information, but if that information is true and constructive, it can be incredibly helpful and not just for the person hearing the information. Because sharing can grow a bond between people, it benefits both the speaker and listener. Millennials want to know they are working for a person, for values, not just for some random corporation that happens to give them benefits.

If you are in management, spend time sitting and chatting with your staff individually. Ask them questions, but try to stay away from anything too personal because they will share it with you whether you want to know it or not! This generation responds positively to genuine concern. Sending messages when someone is sick, or asking how someone is, really goes a long way to keeping a team productive.

Forming mini-families at work seems counter to the business model of the past, which was about money and getting production up. Today if you want production up, money isn't nearly as big a motivating factor as not disappointing family!

There are certain boundaries that still need to be upheld, I don't want you to think I'm saying that you need to be everyone's best friend at work because that is counterproductive. However, letting your Millennials know that they have management staff that cares about them, holistically, can really bring a team together. And once a team Forms, Storms, and Norms—it can then Perform. You'll want to get to that level as fast as possible, and the quickest way is to create safe environments where you can say things like: "Can I be honest with you?" or "Let me be real for a second."

4. Choices that motivate

Remember all of these Millennials were given a trophy for just participating in sports and events at school, so giving awards often, as well as incentives for working on projects or accomplishing tasks, will be beneficial. These don't have to be gift cards or financial rewards, they can be donations to charities in the recipient's name or a variety of other creative ideas. Never underestimate the power of travel. Giving away trips—even simple staycations—can make a happy and healthy workforce. All the workplace research that has come out in the last 10 to 20 years has had a lot to say about incentives. For example, incentives, in and of themselves, don't always work. They may need to be partnered with choice. If a person has a choice and is offered an incentive, then typically they will do whatever is asked to get the incentive.

If a bonus, a gift card, or some other type of monetary reward is dangled over employees' heads, they might respond at first, but the incentive won't work for long. There is only so much someone will do for monetary gain, and since we have already discussed how this generation feels about money, it only makes sense that money is not enough to get them to work harder or smarter. There has to be some sort of buy-in, whether it is a donation or even giving workers options as to what they get if they meet certain goals. It feels less like bribery when workers get to choose. Try it and see if it works for you. A lot of companies, including ones like GoDaddy and Google, have started providing free meals and mid-shift giveaways, which can be fun ways to engage your workers. Your goal is productivity, and their goal is to earn their next trophy, so figuring out ways to make those two objectives meet is the key.

When I taught senior English in high school, I used to give stickers to kids who got their vocabulary worksheets done correctly. You would be amazed at how many kids would come back in the afternoon to show me their corrections, just so they could get a sticker! It's all about finding your particular group's currency and what they care about. Once you discover those, everyone gets a trophy—and you get the most productive group you have ever worked with.

5. Simple steps can change the world

Being a part of something bigger is a great way to get to the heart of people. It can help them not to feel like a cog in a wheel but to see the wheel, or the bigger picture it actually represents. Create causes! Make work and tasks about a cause and follow through. Create campaigns to do good and allow the typically menial tasks to mean something more.

This is something that I discovered when I was an educator. If I made simple tasks into causes that had greater significance, I, as a teacher, could get a greater buy-in and have more participation than we could imagine. The students used to walk around the neighborhood of the school and pick up trash. At first no one liked it. The students complained about being the trash pickers. Once the students learned about how neighbors had been suspicious of the students since the building of the high school in the neighborhood, and how something as simple as picking up trash made the neighbors feel safe and a part of the school, the students saw a mission. They weren't just picking up the trash—they were giving the school a new name with the neighbors. They were including the school in the neighborhood, not keeping the two separate. Even better than that, students who walked to school started picking up trash on their way because they knew they might have to pick it up later anyway and why not be proactive?

We had a flood of emails and calls from the houses around the school, telling us what they had noticed and seen. "I've never seen students pick up trash that wasn't theirs and care so much about the neighborhood." Or even "What are you teaching them over there? I am so impressed with your students." It was simple: we were teaching them about a cause that they needed to be a part of. Once they saw the importance, it was hard to stop them. Find a cause your group can get behind and make your goals match the cause's. How is your group going to save the world one piece of trash at a time—or one TPS report at a time?

6. Harnessing technology

Utilize the Millennials' understanding of technology. Put them in charge of things that are technologically advanced. There is nothing worse than a manager or leader trying to figure out how to use PowerPoint in front of a room of expert techies, who could have been taking care of that part for them.

It took close to 30 years for the telephone to catch on and get into most households in the late 1890's. It took nearly 20 years for color television to become mainstream soon after. Consider that 100 years after the initial adoption of the telephone, society adopted the cell phone (which allowed us to leave the house and still talk on the phone), and today most of us have smartphones (which let us make calls, send text messages, receive and send emails, surf the Internet and get directions). The time it takes for technology to catch on with the masses seems to be getting less and less.

When something new comes out today, because of the information available, Millennials are already waiting in line to buy it, and they learn how to use it in ways no one even knew it was created for. This is why younger and younger generations can catch on to the digital age more quickly than some of us who are older. We have a very valuable resource sitting next to us at the dinner table or in the office. Sometimes, we forget that we can use these younger adults to help us when we don't understand something digital. When we ask them questions, they feel wanted and needed, which can build a stronger and better relationship.

Nearly one-third of Millennials have put off getting married or having a baby due to the recession.

7. I know somebody who can help with that

Take advantage of Millennials' networking abilities. This generation knows a good deal of people and has many connections. When throwing an event or looking for more workers, utilize these advantages and ask for their help. You didn't just hire them for one reason, so use them for more than just one skill or task. Requests that are out of the box and not the usual can really help boost morale and make workers feel they are valued. In my first year of teaching, I had an office that was connected to the classroom.

One day I discovered that someone had gone into my office and taken my iPod, which I used for all my music. I shared the room with a few other teachers so I put the word out. I also told one of my classes how frustrated I was that someone would do that. I had a student come up to me afterward and ask me what sort of iPod it was. I told him, and he put his arm around me and told me he would take care of it. At the time, I wasn't really sure what he was talking about, and he always made great boasts about who he knew, so I sort of brushed it off. A few days later… there was an iPod sitting on my desk, but it was the wrong color and it had music on it that I had never heard of. I brought it to the student and said, "Where did you get this from?" He just shook his head like he had no clue. So I gave it back to him and told him that I didn't want this one and he needed to give it back to whomever he had gotten it from.

It did make me realize that younger kids today have vast networks of people from all over, who are willing to go to great lengths to help their friends out if they are asked. This is a large and fast responding network that we can take advantage of, if and when we get the chance. How can you let the people in your office know what help you need? You will be astonished at how many people know someone that can help out the group in some sort of way. That is what being an office family is all about, is it not? So think or brainstorm with other managers about ways you can tie these networks in to help out your business. The best resource you have is your fellow employees, but you will never know this unless you are able to tap into their network.

8. Multitasking is my middle name

It is hard to be everywhere at once. And being able to do everything at once can be just as tough. For some reason, Millennials have the ability to do many tasks at the same time and do them all very well. It blows my mind when I watch students work on homework, listen to music, and have a conversation with the person next to them, all simultaneously.

Allowing this type of behavior in a work environment can make your younger workers more productive and lets them feel like they can be themselves. Ever walked into a room where teens, especially girls, were studying? What does it look like? Typically, there are three or four of them on opposite sides of the room, music blaring, each of them with a book or two opened in front of them, while they talk on their cell phones. It looks like a mess and, for any of us "older" people, we might go crazy if we stayed in that chaos for more than a few minutes. But to this group, it is the most streamlined and efficient way to get all their work done with the least amount of resistance. They get to hang out with their friends or at least be in the same space with them, which sometimes is all they need. They are communicating with other people from class on their cell phones and keeping up on any news, not just from their friends but also from around the world. Their books are open, and they are able to read through bits of information, pieces at a time—all the while stopping for breaks to sing along with their favorite songs as they come on their computer.

To most of us non-Millennials this environment would be way too distracting. However, if our brains had always processed information from a lot of sources at one time, "chaos" might actually be exactly what we needed to study and work. If we try to keep everything silent when we are asking Millennials to be constantly busy, it doesn't help them get more done. The worst thing that you can do to a student who has attention deficit disorder is to put him (I say "him" because boys make up the majority of people suffering from this diagnosis) in a completely empty room with white walls that have nothing on them. You think he was distracted before? His pencil will start tapping, and his legs will start moving in no time flat. His mind begins to wander, and he can't stop himself because there are *zero* things to stimulate him in the room.

Millennials are often called the ADD generation, so why not let them multitask since that is what they are so good at? Give in to the way they learn and do things. You will love how much they get done on the clock when they are allowed to organize their tasks the way they need them to be. What you call ADD, they call multitasking and they are the experts at it!

A majority of Millennials say that losing their phone or computer has a greater impact on their life than losing their car.

9. Team power

Individuality is something these Millennials hold dear. If you use teams, let them choose who they want to work with. This not only empowers them to choose wisely, but it also will make those teams more successful. Allowing choice can boost morale because group members know that people really wanted to be on their team in the first place instead of being assigned to it. The only way that groups of Millennials can work well together is if they get to choose who they work with.

I have heard several times that Millennials are moving from a "Me" to a "We" generation. I would say that that may be true in most things; however, when it comes to group projects or group work, oftentimes they have had such bad experiences that they would rather work alone and be an individual. So we have to rethink what is group work and what needs to be versus what doesn't. If we allow people to choose which groups they are a part of, it also makes it easier when they complain to us. We didn't assign them to a group; they knew how important it was to choose the right one. So if they chose poorly, then a simple "I'm sorry, I don't know what to do" can be enough to get them to suck it up and get to work. This is a great strategy especially since the desire to choose, and the feeling of empowerment it gives, can be a great way to take some of the small less dramatic decisions out of the hands of the managers. This eliminates some of the normal whining about things that may not be that big of a deal. Let the "Me's" turn into "We's."

10. Focus on outcomes and results

General Patton said, "Don't tell people how to do things, tell them what to do and let them surprise you with their results." So stay true to that, don't tell workers how to do every little thing. Let them figure it out, and you will be amazed at the new ways they find to do things. Chances are these might be more efficient than the way people had been doing the same tasks before.

This is great to keep in mind anytime you work with this generation. Innovation is one of the things that Millennials do best. They can look at a situation and come up with great ways to innovate tasks. Giving them an hour to brainstorm can pay off in major ways later on...when it takes them half the amount of time to get something done. This generation has come up with businesses that could have existed a hundred years ago but haven't. Why? Because people weren't as willing to think outside the box as we are today.

There's a company that donates a pair of eyeglasses to someone in need for every pair of eyeglasses that a customer buys. There is even a company, called Couch Surfing, whose sole design is to provide couches in people's living rooms...for other people (they don't know), who are visiting the area. Companies like Airbnb and Uber are dreams come true for this generation because they are the answer to expensive impersonal experiences. The goal of big hotels and taxis is for everyone to have the exact same experience...a Millennial's worst nightmare. They would rather stay at someone's house, who is out of town for the weekend, no matter what the cost, as long as it provides them with a good experience and lends some sort of character to their stay. That is how Airbnb got started. It's an app on a phone or a computer website that links you with people who are renting a room, or their entire place, while you are in the area.

These types of businesses are making enemies of hotel chains and taxi services, but, in reality, they are taking advantage of a capitalistic society by thinking about things that others would have never thought of. Allow your employees to be creative and innovate the way things are done. Who knows, you may find a new way to be productive or create processes you never knew you needed!

A majority of Millennials admit to not adhering to social media policies in the workplace.

Summing it all up

I understand that you may still have many unanswered questions. To be honest, there are still unexplored aspects of the Millennial generation. It's a complex group that is just starting to enter our workforce and our economic market. There is a lot more that we will learn in the next five to ten years about how they tick. The important thing is that we keep allowing ourselves to grow. If we are open to growing, and we accept and learn from this generation, we will be more successful.

I have seen far too many companies that refuse to change and, with that refusal, they will be bent and some will be broken under the weight of this new generation's needs and demands. Do not be one of those companies! Do not be one of those managers, and do not be one of those who refuse to change. More than ever, companies must be willing to be more organic so they can change with what comes. It's better for our companies, it's better for our stockholders and, in the end, it's better for our economic health.

BY
2030
MILLENNIALS
OUT NUMBER
BOOMERS
BY
22
MILLION

Real True Life Stories
(I promise, they really did happen)

Todd

A 19-year-old, named Todd, was manning the phones at a local cable company when Sam called in hoping to get his new television set up with his existing cable wiring.

TODD: Hello! Thank you for calling your local cable service. How can I help you?

SAM: I need to set up a new television to my existing cable service.

TODD: OK, that's not a problem.

SAM: Great!

(Sounds innocent and decent enough…but here is where the inability to filter and have healthy disclosure happens.)

TODD: Did you put your cable cord in?

SAM: Yup.

TODD: Did you put it in nice and slow? Or quick and hard?

SAM: Ummmm…huh?

TODD: I'm just kidding man.

SAM: I don't think that's funny!

TODD: Well you're no fun!

SAM: Can I talk to your supervisor?

*Click

Trisha

A 23-year-old, named Trisha, had a seasonal job she enjoyed, working with children who had special needs. She hadn't finished her degree and was taking a break to find herself. There was an opening at the end of the season for a full-time person, and she really wanted to apply for it. Her boss made an announcement: "If you want to apply for the full-time management position, please have your résumé on my desk by the end of next week."

At the end of the week there were several résumés on the desk, however, none were Trisha's. When the boss asked Trisha about her résumé, she said, "Oh I can email that to you real fast." The boss reiterated that the process needed to be followed, but it was too late. She got incredibly frustrated and didn't understand why it was such a big deal.

Trisha later went around telling everyone she worked with how unfair it was that they didn't make an exception for her. Once that got back around to the management, there was no way they were going to make an exception for her.

Tina

Tina, who is 19 and works in retail, consistently shows up late to work. Not majorly late, just 15 minutes for three out of five shifts a week. Whenever her manager comes to her and asks her why she's late, she has a myriad of excuses, "Traffic was bad" or "I had to take something to my mom" or "My dog threw up." Finally her manager sat her down and told her that it was an issue, and she said, "But when I'm here, I'm really good so doesn't that cancel it out?"

Jennie

Jennie was fresh out of a big corporate job. She had a degree in accounting and wanted to work at a much smaller company. She sat down at her job interview with a small accounting company in Denver. The interview went well, but the entire time she was waiting for her turn to ask her questions. It was a very important question to her. One that she wished she had asked at her last company. Finally the time had come…her one important question…would it be about her retirement plan or maybe her salary?

Jennie asked, "What do we do for social time with everyone? Do we have regular happy hours or parties in the office?"

The interview committee had to pick their jaws up off the floor.

I didn't include these stories as a way for people to look negatively on the Millennial generation, but rather I wanted to include real-life stories from managers I know personally. I am sure that you recognize some of these stories and have plenty of your own. These types of scenarios happen all the time and can be fixed when we change how we do business with this generation. When we are mindful of the nuances of the Millennial generation we won't be as surprised by their antics, and if there is one thing I don't like in business it's surprises!

Meet the Author

Adam Lee Brooks

Speaker, Author, and Consultant

Adam Lee Brooks

As a first generation college student, Adam has earned a Bachelor's of Science in speech communications, a Masters of Arts in special education, and a Graduate Diploma in leadership development.

Adam founded YAS (Youth Awareness and Safety) as a way to prepare and train adults to train youth. Adam speaks to teens and adults across the country regarding healthy communication, bullying, and body image. He has spoken at assemblies, conferences, and camps where his story of hope and appreciation for one's self continues to transform those he talks to.

With Adam's humor and theatrical style, audiences are entertained as well as moved by his heart-touching stories of life and how we can begin to see ourselves in a healthy and exciting light. Adam's work as an educator and speaker has touched many audiences, young and old while enabling them to Laugh, Reflect and Grow.

For Booking or Consulting, please contact:

Adam Brooks

www.adamleebrooks.com

For more questions about Millennials, please contact:

Adam Brooks

www.youthawarenessandsafety.org